Empath Healing

Survival Guide for Empaths, Become a Healer Instead of Absorbing Negative Energies

Table of Contents

Introduction

Being an empath can be something that is both truly wonderful and scary all at the same time. All too often the special abilities that an empath possesses can cause as many problems as they can help to solve. One of the main differences between empaths who struggle and those who thrive is a deeper understanding of what it means to be an empath. This book will explore the true nature of being an empath, as well as the different types of empathic abilities that exist. This will help you not only determine if you are an empath, but it will reveal the exact type of empath you are. Furthermore, this book will provide useful information with how to hone and harness your empathic skills, thereby helping you to get the most from your abilities. It will also explore several methods for helping you to stay grounded, thus preventing your empathic nature from taking you too far from the physical plane. By the time you finish reading this book you will not only be able to decide what your abilities are, you will also know how to use them in a way that is fulfilling, enriching and that creates the wonderful life that you deserve.

Chapter 1: What Is an Empath?

The term ‘empath' is one that has become more commonly recognized in recent years for several different reasons. Most people probably know the term from pop culture sources, such as TV, movies and even literature. There have been numerous fictional characters to receive the moniker ‘empath,' although the accuracy of their portrayal is a matter of debate. Another reason why many people are familiar with the term is an increase in the popularity of personality tests. While some of these tests focus on personality traits as defined by psychology, others focus on other traits, such as psychic abilities, spiritual paths and the like. It is among these personality tests that the empath name is used to define a specific type of person, namely someone who is highly in tune with their intuition. Needless to say, how an empath is defined differs widely from one source to another, leaving the average person asking the simple question, "What is an empath?" This chapter will address some of the common misconceptions of empaths, while also presenting the basic characteristics that actually make up what an empath truly is.

Popular misconceptions of an empath

Empaths in popular culture cover a whole range of characteristics, abilities and personality traits. Although most of these depictions are positive in nature, many are highly exaggerated, if not completely baseless and unrealistic. This stands to reason since most movies, TV shows and books are more interested in creating exciting, alluring characters rather than exploring the true makeup of a real-life empath. Nevertheless, it is important to understand the difference between the pop-culture empath and the one that actually exists.

The first misconception is that an empath can read minds like you would read a book. This notion gained significant popularity with the character Deanna Troi from Star Trek the Next Generation. In the show, Deanna Troi came from a race of empaths known as Betazoids. Members of this race could not only read minds, but they could communicate with each other telepathically as well. Deanna was only half Betazoid, however, meaning that her powers were only half as strong. Ironically, she was only able to sense strong emotions due to her mixed heritage, which actually makes her more of a true empath than the show's depiction of people who are basically telepathic.

Another misconception in pop-culture is that empaths somehow completely understand their ability and fully know how to use it. All too often an empath will not only sense danger, but they will know that what they are feeling is a warning, not merely a reaction to the environment, something they heard or even something they ate. Even when they are in the midst of a conversation or an event they are actively engaged in they are able to easily distinguish between the emotions of others and their own emotional experience. Furthermore, they always know the exact meaning of the emotional red flag they are receiving, making it seem as if the universe was whispering in their ear. Unfortunately, this isn't how it works.

Some characters take the intuitive capabilities of an empath to a whole new level, going as far as being able to foresee future or faraway events. This can be seen in Star Wars, where Jedi Masters 'use the force' to assess a situation on an intuitive level. Needless to say, being able to sense far off disasters, know when the bad guy is in town or any other similar scenario is a real stretch at best. What is ironic in this instance is that Han Solo more accurately portrays a true empath when he says his iconic line "I have a bad feeling about this." While there is a great deal of debate over just how far a person's empathic abilities can go, the bottom line is that the average empath relies solely on whether a choice or situation feels good or bad.

Finally, there is the fanciful idea that all empaths have mystical personalities, speaking in riddles and hearing the voice of the universe in all living things. Needless to say, this isn't really the way it is. That isn't to suggest that there isn't at least a kernel of truth to this depiction, however, merely that it is so exaggerated as to be virtually unrecognizable from reality. The bottom line is that you may never realize that a person is empathic by their overall personality since many appear as normal as anyone else. Empaths who are more in tune with their emotions may seem more mystical since they are more inwardly focused than the average person. Alternatively, they may seem less mystical and more self-absorbed or even just detached. Thus, the idea that empaths have their own language and recognize each other by their aura is complete fiction and should be recognized as such.

The true nature of an empath

Just because the pop-culture depiction of empaths is exaggerated and fantastic doesn't mean to suggest that empaths aren't actually something to be admired. The fact of the matter is that a confident, well-functioning empath is someone who stands out from the crowd, not only in terms of personality but also in terms of ability. Although empaths need to use spoken words to communicate and they don't hear the voice of the universe as such, they still possess certain skills, which can make them seem otherworldly at times.

One ability common to empaths is that of being able to get an accurate first impression of a person. This is a skill that just about anyone would pay good money to acquire. While it may not be as flashy as telepathy or predicting the future it can go a long way to avoiding getting taken advantage of by would-be con artists and the like. The biggest problem with first impressions is that most people try to 'impress' you when you meet them. They will be friendlier than normal, more poised than normal and will leave you believing that they are capable and trustworthy overall. Empaths, however, are not so easily fooled. Rather than relying on the physical senses to determine a person's character, empaths use their intuition. This means that they see past the words a person says, sensing what lies beneath.

This leads to another real aspect of empaths – trust issues. These aren't the usual trust issues between one person and another, rather they are the issues faced when an empath's intuition is telling them something completely different from what their rational mind is telling them. First impressions are a great example of this conflict. Again, most people put on their best appearance when meeting someone for the first time, and this can make them seem super friendly, highly reliable and generally very decent. While this can fool the intellect, such a show can never fool intuition. As a result, an empath can get two first impressions of a person, the one they think and the one they feel. The challenge is in believing the intuitive impression. After all, it's very difficult to trust a bad feeling about a person who appears completely safe and good. Subsequently, many empaths struggle with trusting those feelings that defy outward appearances.

Another common skill among empaths is the ability to sense the energy of a situation. At first this may seem like something from pop-culture, however, it actually makes more sense when you examine it closely. The main tool that an empath uses is their intuition. This intuition can sense the emotions of another person, making them as real as the empath's own emotions. That said, any situation contains a particular energy of its own, made up of the energies of all people involved in the situation. It's a bit like noise. A single person speaking will make a certain amount of noise, noise that your ears can easily hear. Likewise, a crowd of people talking will make similar noise, albeit louder and more chaotic due to how many conversations are going on. Nevertheless, your ears can easily hear that noise too. Energy acts in the very same way. An empath can sense the energy of an individual, as well as the energy of a situation. In this way they can sense when a situation is negative in any way, such as dangerous or potentially sinister.

In the end, an empath is simply someone who has a more heightened intuition, which enables them to perceive things that the physical senses cannot perceive. While this may seem mystical and otherworldly to some, it is commonplace for those with the ability. Although this ability can have many positive applications the sad truth is that it can cause as many problems as it can potentially solve. Thus, as well as being highly gifted, empaths are usually quite conflicted, making their lives extra challenging as well as extra special.

Chapter 2: Are You an Empath?

The chances are you aren’t reading this book because you wanted to better understand what an empath is. Instead, you are probably reading this book because you want to better understand *who you are*. Although the last chapter only touched on some of the basic elements of what an empath is and what an empath isn't you may have resonated with enough to move on to the next question – namely, are you an empath? This chapter will list sixteen different questions that will help you to discover whether or not you are a real-life empath. As you read each question take the time to carefully consider your answer. The more accurate your answers are, the more accurate the conclusion will be. So, without further ado, let's see if you are in fact a bona fide empath! Are you/do you:

Prone to bouts of anxiety or depression?

Anxiety and depression are key signs of an empath, specifically because they are so in tune with their emotions. While most people are focused on the external world, empaths are usually wholly focused on their internal world. This makes them far more susceptible to extreme moods, both positive and negative. While others can find countless things to distract them from their emotional state, empaths are constantly aware of their emotions. Thus, it's not as though empaths are necessarily more emotional than everyone else, rather it's that they are more aware of their emotional condition at any given time.

Another reason why empaths are prone to bouts of anxiety or depression is the constant flow of emotional traffic they have to deal with. Just as the average person can hear the noise of the people around them an empath can feel the emotions of those around them. Many people tune out noise by putting on headphones or ear buds and listening to music. Unfortunately, empaths can't just tune out emotional input that easily. As a result, they feel all of the stress and anxiety of those around them in addition to their own emotional state. Needless to say, this increase in stressful energy is enough to create real problems.

While depression is a fairly natural condition, experienced by most people from time to time, empaths can tend to suffer from it on a more regular basis. One reason for this, as with stress and anxiety, is that an empath can feel the depression of others. Overexposure to other people's depression can impact an empath's emotional state in a very negative way. The easiest way to tell the difference between normal depression and empathic depression is context. If you feel depressed for no reason, meaning that no event or trauma has caused you to feel that way, then you might be an empath.

Overwhelmed in crowded places such as the movies or the mall?

Many people love to go to malls and other places in order to experience the energy of large crowds of people who are having fun. In a way they get inspired by such high energy environments. Other people, however, aren't as fond of crowds and their energy. This is especially true of empaths. The number one reason for this is that the more people an empath is around is the more emotional input they are subjected to. Just as the chaos and noise of a crowd can cause a normal person's mind to spin out of control, the emotional energy of a crowd can cause an empath's entire being to spin out of control. Therefore, if you feel overwhelmed in crowded places you might be an empath.

This isn't to say that you have to hate crowded places altogether. There are times when an empath can get their batteries charged from crowded places, although these are very specific circumstances. An event that induces generally positive energy is an example of this. Such events can include concerts or other situations that lack anxiety due to competition, frustration and the like. This is why sporting events can be dangerous since they can generate as much tension and stress as any positive feelings. However, even the most positive crowd is a crowd nonetheless, and many empaths struggle with exposure to crowds of any kind.

Drawn to healing, helping and care-giving fields?

More often than not the metrics used to determine the empathic nature of a person are negative in nature. However, there are just as many positive metrics that can be used as well. One such metric is whether or not you are drawn to fields of healing, helping and care-giving. Being in tune with other people's emotions makes an empath highly aware of another person's pain and suffering. Subsequently, any job that helps to alleviate pain and suffering would be a natural draw to an empath. Therefore, if you find that you are allured to such professions as the medical field, psychology, relationship counseling and the like you are probably an empath.

This might seem like a bit of a paradox since placing an empath in such an environment would place them under extreme emotional stress. Unfortunately, this is one of the dangers inherent with empaths seeking such jobs. By getting emotionally attached to the people they help, empaths can become emotionally drained very quickly on a regular basis. Even so, the process of improving a person's health and wellbeing seems to compensate for this, since a person's emotional state improves with their physical and psychological state. This is why empaths can function well in such environments. Therefore, if you are the type of person who feels better when other people feel better, you just might be an empath!

Sensitive to the emotions of others during childhood?

Childhood is challenging enough for just about everyone. Empaths, as you might by now expect, have an even tougher time. This is because in addition to having to deal with the emotional volatility of being a child, empaths have the added burden of sensing the emotions of the people around them. One way that this manifests is in the area of guilt. As a child you no doubt did numerous things that upset your parents. The average child would feel somewhat guilty for such wrongdoings, however, an empath will feel enormous guilt. This is because you can sense the pain or anger of your parents. If every falling out with your parents was an emotional tidal wave for you it probably means you had the tough task of growing up as an empath.

Another sign that a child is an empath is the number of people who confide in them. The simple truth is that by feeling other people's emotions an empath can understand exactly what that person is going through. Such an understanding makes them seem years wiser than they should be. As a result, people of all ages are drawn to them, sharing their deep secrets as well as regrets, hopes, fears and every other important thought or feeling that they might have. If you experienced such incidents of others opening their souls to you it means you were recognized for your empathic abilities even at a young age.

Prefer time in nature, alone or with animals over being with people?

This question is related to the one regarding crowds. The thing with crowds is that a person can hate them without being an empath. However, if you prefer time alone, in nature or with animals instead of being with other people, then you are probably an empath. This is especially true if you hate being in crowds too!

Empaths love nothing more than a long, peaceful walk in nature. Understandably, the main reason for this is the lack of human interaction. Although it is widely known that even trees and plants give off energy, the fact is that this energy is of a different nature to that of human emotions. The energy in nature is calming, refreshing and rejuvenating in essence, meaning that it restores a person rather than wearing them down. As a result, empaths are usually drawn to nature, even choosing to live in more rural areas in order to surround themselves with nature's restorative energies.

Animals, like nature, lack the emotional complexity and chaos of people. Subsequently, empaths will usually choose to spend more time with animals than they will with other people. At first glance this may seem antisocial in nature, however, it simply comes down to a matter of self preservation. While empaths enjoy time alone they can become depressed when isolated for too long. Animals can be the perfect solution by providing non-human company that takes the loneliness out of solitude. As a result, many empaths have cats or dogs in their lives that they lavish with love and affection.

Finally, there is the aspect of alone time. Some people cannot stand being alone for long periods, finding the solitude and quiet as disturbing as empaths find noise and crowds. In contrast, an empath will not only desire alone time, they will actually need it in order to stay balanced. If an empath is deprived of time alone their stress levels will begin to rise dramatically, reaching dangerous levels if the situation persists. Empaths can become emotionally volatile as a result, lashing out in fits of anger and rage at even the slightest of things. Alternatively, they can express their emotional fatigue through bouts of crying that come on unexpectedly and for no apparent reason. All that is needed to set things right again is a decent dose of solitude. If this sounds like you, you are almost definitely an empath.

Struggle with establishing boundaries or saying "No" to others?

A common phenomenon found within anyone who possesses an inherent skill or talent is that they also possess the corresponding desire to put that talent to use. This is particularly evident in the case of empaths. More often than not, empaths will not only attract those with difficulties who need someone to confide in, they will also actively seek out such people.

Unfortunately, this can lead to a problem that manifests within most empaths, namely the inability to say "no."

If you struggle with establishing boundaries, or simply saying "no" to those in need you aren't gullible or spineless, rather you are probably an empath. The fact is that by feeling the pain of others you take on the need to comfort and resolve that pain. Therefore, no matter how tired you are you will always commit to helping someone in need. Furthermore, you will probably give of yourself on a level that most people would draw the line on. This takes the form of lending people money, even when you barely have enough for yourself, letting someone move into your home or any other form of help that serves to affect your life in a very real way. If any of these situations seems familiar it probably indicates that you are a true empath.

Tend to feel drained by the people in your life?

Most people like to spend time with others in order to restore their energies. This can take the form of large and loud parties, or it can come in the form of smaller, more intimate gatherings. Either way, most people come away from social interactions feeling more energized than when they went in. In the case of an empath, however, the opposite is usually true. Rather than feeling energized by others, empaths will tend to feel drained by the people in their lives.

One of the main reasons for this is that people either send energy out or they take energy in. You can think of this as either being a radio transmitter or a radio receiver. Those who are receivers soak up the energy of those around them, becoming stronger and more vibrant as a result. In contrast, those who send energy out become drained by those around them, especially when most of them are receivers rather than transmitters. Empaths are a strange breed, possessing both the ability to transmit as well as the ability to receive. Thus, they can come away from a social gathering having absorbed all of the negative energy while also having transmitted all of their positive energy to everyone else. As a result, empaths will usually feel drained by the people in their life.

Experience random mood swings?

Random mood swings are a common symptom of any empath, causing them to seem quirky at best and emotionally unstable at worst. The main reason these mood swings cause concern amongst non-empaths is that they occur for no apparent reason. Most people judge life by what their physical senses perceive, therefore things are always as they appear. Empaths, in contrast, experience life on an emotional level, meaning that they perceive the unseen energies that underlie physical reality. As a result, empaths can become overwhelmed by negative energies that the average person can't sense, let alone see. This can cause an empath to have instant and unexplained mood swings anytime, anywhere.

The most common of these mood swings is sadness or depression. When an empath is in the presence of stress, anxiety and sorrow their demeanor will take on those traits. Even though they aren't unhappy themselves, an empath can't help but absorb the energy around them. Thus, their mood will change depending on their environment. If this happens to you, don't be alarmed, rather than being unstable you are actually demonstrating a trait of being an empath.

Feel the emotions of others, as though the experience is yours?

A common misconception about empaths is that they are simply regular people who feel a deeper sense of sympathy for those who are suffering. This understanding, or rather misunderstanding, is what causes so much frustration amongst those who want to help empaths when they are feeling overwhelmed. What the average person fails to understand is that there is a huge difference between sympathy and empathy. Feeling sympathy is when you feel bad for someone else who is suffering. Empathy, on the other hand, is when you actually feel the emotions of others, as though those emotions were your own. This means that you actually share the experience on an emotional level, even though you don't on the physical level. Which is why, as an empath, you have a hard time walking away from those in need.

Although this trait usually manifests itself in a negative way, causing an empath to share the pain, sorrow and suffering of others, it can also manifest itself in a more positive way. Empaths can also share in the joy and excitement that others feel. Such circumstances, although rarer in nature, can go a long way to restoring an empath's energies. As a result, many empaths have learned to seek out environments where the emotional charge is positive in order to balance and restore their own emotional wellbeing.

Have a general need for solitude?

More often than not an empath will find themselves in an environment that is defined by such negative emotions as fear, sorrow, anger and stress. This is due to the fact that these emotions are much stronger than contentment or peace, therefore they overwhelm any environment the same way a bad smell can overwhelm the air of a large room. As a result, empaths have a general need for solitude. By spending time alone an empath can not only avoid negative energies from the outside, but they can also take the time to discover the true condition of their own emotional state. This allows them to recognize any issues they have to address in their lives in order to restore balance and wellbeing to their hearts and minds.

Another reason why empaths need solitude is just to stop the flow of emotional energy from the outside. Needless to say, the constant flow of negative energy that bombards an empath can leave them feeling depressed and drained. However, positive energy can also have that effect after a while. In a way it's a bit like noise. Even the most pleasant of noises can become irritating after a while, causing a person to seek out silence in order to rest their ears. Likewise, solitude serves the purpose of soothing an empath's mind from any and all energy. If you are drawn to solitude there is a good chance it's because you are an empath.

Experience anxiety from noise, smells and excessive talkers?

Although empaths experience life on an emotional level, this doesn't mean that they don't use their physical senses just like everyone else. On the contrary, not only are empaths acutely aware of their physical senses, but the input received from these senses can impact an empath more than the average person. While sensory input usually goes straight to the intellectual mind of the average person, the same input goes straight to the emotional mind of the empath. This means that instead of analyzing this input an empath feels it. The word most commonly used to describe this state is sensitivity. As a result, most empaths are far more sensitive to such things as noise, smells and excessive talking.

If you find that you become easily stressed and anxious from strong odors, loud noise or the constant chatter of non-stop talking this suggests that you are probably an empath. This can actually cause nausea in the case of smells, seeing as you are more sensitive to such input. However, the most common physiological effects are headache, panic attacks and general irritability. This is because your heart rate is increased, as is your adrenaline production. After a while these factors will begin to cause your body and mind to become agitated, so much so that you will be unable to focus or think clearly until you are able to find a place of solitude where you can recover your emotional equilibrium.

Adversely affected by bright lights?

In addition to smells, sounds and excessive talking, bright lights can also cause a great deal of distress to an empath. Again, this is due to an empath's increased sensitivity to sensory input. When exposed to bright lights for a short time an empath can feel a bit disoriented, agitated or just anxious due to an increase in adrenaline. However, if the exposure is prolonged, or the light is extremely bright, an empath may experience symptoms as extreme as migraines, heart palpitations or even nausea. Unfortunately, the correlation between such symptoms and bright light is not something that most people would think of, resulting in empaths being misdiagnosed or simply undiagnosed altogether.

When you understand how such conditions affect an empath the symptoms become much easier to recognize and address. If you ever feel this way in brightly lit environments you need to take action as soon as possible. Needless to say, the first choice would be to remove yourself from the environment altogether. However, if this isn't possible you should do what you can to reduce the effects of bright light. A good option is to carry a pair of softly tinted sunglasses that will reduce the light without making indoor environments too dark. Simply knowing why you have the symptoms is only half the battle. Taking care of yourself when those symptoms occur is the other, and perhaps most important half.

Have a hard time going to sleep before midnight?

Sometimes empaths can demonstrate symptoms that are shared with other personality types. Insomnia, for example, is one such symptom. Most people link insomnia with an overactive mind, especially the type associated with such personalities as problem solvers, inventors and even worriers. While these personalities do experience insomnia on a fairly regular basis they aren't the only ones. Empaths can have a hard time going to sleep, usually as a result of the emotional overload they experience during the day. Such an overload increases stress and anxiety, which in turn makes it harder to fall asleep and drift off into peaceful, contented slumber.

One of the easiest ways to tell the difference between empath insomnia and the other forms is the amount of activity going on in the conscious mind. Inventors and problem solvers will struggle with sleep since their brains are mulling over details about plans, projects or the like, thus keeping their minds too active for sleep. Even worriers will be playing their greatest fears over and over again in their minds, thus keeping them from peaceful sleep. However, an empath can have trouble falling asleep even though their conscious mind is relatively calm and at peace. This suggests an emotional cause rather than an intellectual one. If this sounds like you it means you are probably an empath.

Feel the presence of otherworldly spirits?

This might be a topic you have trouble sharing with the people in your life, especially those who aren't empaths. After all, how many people in your life would react well to you telling them that you can feel the presence of otherworldly spirits?! Unfortunately, as already discussed, most people experience life through their physical senses alone, meaning that their experience is limited to those things that can be seen, heard, touched, smelled and tasted. While there have been numerous reports of spirits creating smells, temperature changes and the like, the chances are the average person wouldn't be sensitive enough to recognize such signs, let alone realize what they actually meant.

Fortunately (or unfortunately, depending on your point of view), empaths are capable of perceiving otherworldly spirits through non-physical means. Since spirits are made up of energy, it stands to reason that empaths can sense them the same way they sense other people's emotions. The biggest problem is in not knowing what such sensations are all about, which can create significant distress and anxiety in an empath who senses a spirit without understanding the event. That said, if you have ever felt 'not alone,' don't panic. You aren't having a mental breakdown, instead you are probably sensing another being that simply lacks physical form.

Love trees, mountains or the ocean?

As you might expect, empaths are often drawn to places where people are in scarce supply. These places include forests, mountains and large bodies of water such as oceans. The obvious reason for being drawn to these places is that it provides an empath with some much needed solitude. By spending time away from people empaths can recharge their emotional batteries, giving them the strength to cope with the emotional overload they will face when they return to society.

There is, however, another reason why empaths love these natural sanctuaries, one that the average person simply wouldn't understand. Places such as mountains and oceans seem to defy humanity, proving the power of nature over the power of man. Oddly enough, empaths tend to find comfort in this truth, feeling a sense of relief that the overwhelming world of man does, in fact, have its limits, limits which cannot be overcome. As a result, forests, mountains and oceans are something of a sacred space for empaths, a space free from human incursion and development.

Go above and beyond in all your relationships?

When it comes to relationships, the tendency for empaths to go above and beyond reaches all new levels. This stands to reason when you consider the fact that empaths are willing to do whatever it takes to rescue perfect strangers from their pain and suffering. How much further will an empath be willing to go in order to rescue a loved one from similar pain and suffering? The answer is quite a lot. Because empaths care even more for the emotional wellbeing of loved ones they will do anything they can to help maintain their relationship with them, even when that effort isn't reciprocated. This is because they know the pain that letting the relationship fail will cause, and if there is one thing an empath cannot do it is willingly cause pain to another person.

Another reason why empaths are so willing to over-invest in relationships, both of a romantic nature as well as platonic relationships, is that they are far more forgiving of any wrongs done to them. Because an empath relates to the emotions of others they also relate to the fallibility of others. Thus, when a romantic partner does something that would drive the average person away, an empath will identify with the action, and thus forgive their partner the way they would want to be forgiven if the roles were reversed. Unfortunately, this often results in empaths remaining in unhealthy relationships for far too long, causing them even greater pain and suffering in the long run. If this has happened to you, then you just might be an empath.

What your answers mean

If you are an empath, the chances are you identified with most, if not all of the questions presented in this chapter. This is because these questions are based on the actions of an empath due to their highly intuitive and emotional nature. However, this doesn't mean that you have to answer 'yes' to all of the questions in order to be a real life empath. Certain questions may apply to one type of empath over another, so answering 'no' to some of the questions doesn't take away from the chances of you being an empath. In short, if you identify with at least half of the scenarios described you are doubtlessly an empath. The next question to answer is exactly what type of empath are you?

Chapter 3: General Types of Empaths

Being an empath is a bit like being an artist. While art is fundamentally about self-expression there are many forms that it takes, such as painting, sculpture, dance and the like. The same can be said for empaths. Although the fundamental reality of being an empath remains fairly the same, there are several different types of empath that a person can be. The questions in the last chapter can help to narrow down which type of empath you are, however it can be easier to make that determination by comparing each of the types against your own experience. This chapter will discuss six different types of empath, showing which qualities are unique to each. With this information you will be able to identify the exact form of empathy that you possess, and how it can apply to your day-to-day life.

Emotional Empath

Emotional empaths are the most common type of empath, and the most basic. This is the variation that most people identify with when they think of the term 'empath.' As an emotional empath you will be able to sense the emotions of those around you, thereby knowing what a person is feeling regardless of their outward appearance. The ease with which you can sense the emotions of others can be both a blessing and a curse. Although it can be a good thing to know what another person is truly feeling, the truth is that you can sense the emotions of others as easily as you sense your own feelings. This can make it difficult to differentiate between the two at times, causing a fair amount of emotional confusion as a result.

To say that you can sense other people's emotions may actually be understating your experience somewhat. The fact is that you cannot only sense how others are feeling, but you can share in those feelings as well. Again, this can cause significant confusion with regard to your actual emotional state. You will probably experience mood swings as a result of how others are feeling, and this can make you seem unstable in extreme cases. Subsequently, it is important to develop the ability to differentiate between the emotions of others and your own feelings. This will help you to stay true to your emotional state regardless of the environment you are in. Additionally, by remaining detached you can prove more beneficial when helping those around you since you aren't allowing your own energies to be altered or drained by their emotional experience.

Physical/Medical Empath

The second type of empath is the physical/medical empath. If you possess this type of empathy you will be able to sense another person's physical health and wellbeing. Essentially, the experience is the same as with an emotional empath, however, instead of being able to tap into another person's emotional state you are able to tap into their physiological state. One way this takes shape is that you get an image or a sense of something that is wrong. For example, if someone has a chronic illness, such as diabetes, the word 'diabetes' might appear in your mind, seemingly out of nowhere. Alternatively, you might actually be able to feel the symptoms of another person the same way an emotional empath can feel another person's emotions. This can be very distressing if you don't know what is going on since you may experience numerous symptoms throughout any given day, even though you are in perfect health yourself.

Some physical/medical empaths can actually see issues in another person's energy, such as blockages, imbalances and the like. This is where practices such as Reiki can prove a very beneficial profession, as such an empath could use their abilities to detect and help correct a person's energy issues. For the most part, people in this category choose medical professions where they can use their intuition to help diagnose and cure the patients they see. Needless to say, the same detachment that can benefit emotional empaths can go a long way to benefiting physical/medical empaths as well. After all, you can't be of much use to others if you think the symptoms you feel are yours rather than theirs!

Geomantic Empath

Geomantic empaths are those who can sense the energy of a place, landscape or environment. If you have ever experienced a strong emotional response to being in a place you might be a geomantic empath. However, this is only true in the case that the environment is relatively free of people. After all, if there are many people in an area you might actually be picking up on their energies, which is what an emotional empath would do. Geomantic empaths, in contrast, feel the energy of an environment that is relatively deserted, meaning they are feeling the energy of the place, not of other people.

One example of this can be found in nature. As a geomantic empath you will feel a deeper sadness anytime you witness trees being cut down or patches of natural land being developed for human use. The sorrow you feel for such an event would be similar to the sorrow an average person would feel for a tragedy in which numerous lives were lost. Essentially, as a geomantic empath you identify all life as equally sacred and the fact that you feel the energy of natural environments only strengthens that fact.

There is another form of experience for geomantic empaths, one that involves 'energy fingerprints.' Anytime you feel extremely sad, frightened, happy or angry when you are in a place it could point to the energy imprint left by countless people who had specific experiences in that place. For example, an old jail might make you feel depressed and sad, whereas an old theater might make you feel happy and excited. This is the result of the emotional fingerprint left by those who were there when the place was active. All in all, if you are a geomantic empath it is important that you leave places that make you feel uncomfortable and spend time in places that bring you peace and joy, such as forests, beaches and other natural environments.

Plant Empath

One of the things that most empaths discover at some point in their lives is that the energy that flows through humans is very much the same as the energy that flows through all of nature. Therefore, it will be no surprise to discover that there is an actual form of empathy that specifically focuses on plants. If this form describes you then you are a plant empath. Like a physical/medical empath you are able to sense and identify the physical wellbeing of those around you. However, in this case instead of people it's all about the plants around you. This means you have an intuitive green thumb!

As a plant empath you can feel the actual needs of the plants you come into contact with. To the outsider this can seem as though you are keenly observant, capable of discerning a plant's health by even the most subtle of signs. However, the truth is that you only find those signs because you know what to look for. This can make you very capable working in such places as parks, nurseries, or for any type of landscaping company. Not only will you be able to detect problems early on, but you will also know intuitively how to address those problems, using techniques that most others wouldn't even have thought of.

If you are a plant empath you probably have numerous plants in and around your home. This is because healthy plants give off energy that is rejuvenating to an empath, regardless of type. By nurturing plants to their optimum health you are actually helping to create an environment that benefits you as much as you benefit the plants. Although some might scoff when you talk to your plants or hug your trees you know that such actions are as natural as when two people talk to each other or engage in an embrace.

Animal Empath

Most empaths feel a closer bond to nature, resulting in them having more plants and animals in their lives. However, an animal empath takes this bond to a whole new level. Much like a plant empath, animal empaths are able to sense the condition and needs of any animal they come into contact with. One of the main differences between plants and animals, however, is the depth of communication that can occur between animals and animal empaths. While plants can communicate needs and conditions, animals can communicate feelings, thoughts and even desires. Make no mistake, just because an animal can't express their thoughts with the spoken word doesn't mean that those thoughts don't exist.

If you are an animal empath you will have an almost telepathic ability with any animal you meet. Not only will you be able to sense their feelings and thoughts, you will also be able to transmit your feelings and thoughts to them.

As a result, animal empaths make the best veterinarians, pet sitters and animal psychologists. Most actively seek out jobs in such areas since helping animals is a very real part of an animal empath's design. Furthermore, like physical/medical empaths, animal empaths can detect illnesses in an animal, making it possible to treat animals more quickly and effectively as a result. The only downside is that most animal empaths will become fairly antisocial, choosing to spend their lives with animals over people due to the connection they have with the animal kingdom.

Claircognizant/Intuitive Empath

Finally, there is the type of empath known as the claircognizant/intuitive empath. These empaths are capable of not only sensing the emotions of other people, but of actually perceiving other people on an intuitive level. This means they can receive information from another person just by being around them. Scientific studies have demonstrated the possibility of this phenomenon, specifically as it relates to the actual nature of thoughts. It turns out that thoughts are comprised of energy, making it possible for them to be perceived much the same way that emotions are. The single difference is that claircognizant/intuitive empaths seem to pick up on energies of a more conscious nature, such as thoughts, intentions and personality traits.

The main advantage that claircognizant/intuitive empaths have is that they can perceive a person's true identity quickly and easily. This means that they know what a person is like regardless of outward appearance or even their emotional state. Subsequently, they are able to get the most accurate first impressions of a person. In more extreme cases claircognizant/intuitive empaths can all but read another person's mind, making them virtually telepathic. Unfortunately, this level of perception can easily lead to sensory overload. It is recommended, therefore, that claircognizant/intuitive empaths develop the ability to 'turn off' their abilities at will in order to allow them the ability to recharge their batteries. Additionally, it is advised that they carefully choose the company they keep, ensuring that they spend time with people they can trust and feel comfortable around.

The Takeaway

The chances are one or more of the empath types listed in this chapter resonate with you. Few people possess traits from only one type, meaning that most empaths are a mix of two or more empathic types. You might be an intuitive empath with claircognizant or geomantic tendencies. In the end, the better you understand your abilities, the easier it will be to nurture and use those abilities. Hopefully, this chapter has helped you to not only understand your abilities and experiences better, but to understand yourself in a more meaningful way. Always remember, being an empath is something you should enjoy and be proud of!

Chapter 4: What Areas Does It Affect Our Lives?

Being an empath is something that affects every area of your life. It's not like a job where you clock in, do your work, clock out and go home. The experience of being an empath is one that takes place 24 hours a day, 7 days a week. Subsequently, there is no area of your life that is left unaffected by your empathic abilities. Although you can't prevent your empathic nature from influencing your life you can manage those influences, thereby taking control from the effects of your emotional environment. This chapter will discuss six different areas that are directly affected by empathic abilities, revealing some of the challenges faced as well as ways to overcome them.

Health

One of the most common areas affected by empathic abilities is a person's health. The negative effects of the constant bombardment of emotions can be overwhelming at best and devastating at worst. Although these effects cannot be avoided altogether when a person is aware of them they can make decisions and choices that better protect their wellbeing.

Some of the lesser physical symptoms that empaths frequently suffer from include headaches, fatigue and minor panic attacks. These are usually brought on by long exposure to large crowds, noisy environments or any other situation involving harsh sensory input. Such symptoms fade quickly once the empath finds a quiet place in which to rebalance their energies. In the event that they cannot get away, these symptoms can turn into more extreme forms, including migraine, dizziness, nausea and even muscle pain.

In addition to affecting physical health and wellbeing, empathic abilities can significantly affect a person's emotional health and wellbeing as well. Lesser symptoms include a general feeling of sadness, low energy levels and even mild stress and anxiety. Such symptoms are usually the result of being in a negative environment or around people with negatively charged emotions. They can also be the result of becoming emotionally spent due to helping those in need. If left unchecked, these symptoms can turn into more serious issues, including depression, extreme anxiety and even rage in some cases. Needless to say, it is critical that you find a place of solitude in the event that you start experiencing any of these symptoms, as only then can you begin to undo the harmful effects of your environment. Daily meditation will also help to increase your stamina in highly charged emotional environments.

Addictions

Many empaths find the constant flow of emotional energy that bombards their senses hard to cope with from time to time. While most find healthy ways to deal with these situations others turn to less healthy methods. In fact, some develop addictions in their quest to dull their senses and bring a sense of tranquility to their minds. While some addictions are less harmful than others, the bottom line is that no addiction is truly healthy. Therefore, it is important that you be on the lookout for addictive behavior in your life in order to avoid any long-term, harmful consequences.

One such addiction is eating. This makes a lot of sense when you consider the effects food can have on both the body and the mind. Most eating addictions involve treats or comfort food, things that make a person happy just thinking about them. Thus, not only do foods such as ice cream and cake provide a quick boost of sugary energy, they also create a sense of comfort and peace that helps to restore the mind. From time to time such an indulgence can be healthy, however, when that indulgence turns into addiction it can have very negative effects on both body and mind.

Other addictions include drinking alcohol and smoking. These addictions also make sense seeing as they provide a chemical depressant that helps to dull an empath's senses, thereby relieving them from the inner chaos and turmoil that their mind experiences most of the time. Shopping is another common addiction, one that is less understood than the others. However, it makes perfect sense when you take the time to truly consider it. When a person shops they have the hope and expectation of finding something that will bring joy and fulfillment to their lives. Since empaths often suffer from sadness and even depression, such an expectation will go a long way to raising their spirits. In the end, these addictions are usually nothing more than an empath's way of self-medicating through their more serious bouts of depression and anxiety.

If you experience such addictive behavior it is critical to talk to someone who might be able to help you overcome it. Alternatively, turning to such things as meditation and exercise in place of addictive behavior can actually help replace unhealthy habits with healthier, more beneficial ones.

Relationships, Love, and Sex

Unfortunately, the empathic nature of a person often results in them finding themselves in the midst of toxic relationships that they simply cannot escape. This dynamic has two main reasons. First, empaths are usually drawn to people who need help, seeing as they have an inherent need to offer support and assistance whenever possible. While this seems like a good thing, the fact is that it can result in empaths being attracted to those who are abusive and even self-destructive in nature. The more damaged a person, the more attractive they are to an empath. The second reason is that an empath cannot abandon someone in need. Therefore, even when they realize their relationship is toxic they become stuck as they can't bring themselves to cause suffering to the other person by ending the relationship. Talking to someone, be it a friend or a counselor, can go a long way to resolving this dilemma.

Another way that empaths struggle with relationships is that they are often emotionally spent, meaning that they don't always have the energy needed to nurture a healthy and loving relationship. This doesn't mean that empaths don't crave deep and meaningful relationships, rather they don't usually reserve enough emotional energy to invest in their own happiness, spending it all on the happiness of others instead. The only real solution to this is for an empath to find someone who is both very energetic as well as very understanding with regard to the empath's plight.

Love and sex are also highly impacted by a person's empathic abilities. While many people see sex as an act that expresses love between two people, empaths often see it as a way to deaden their senses, restoring them to a state of being physically grounded. This can cause tension in any relationship where the other person feels more lusted after than loved when it comes to intimacy. The truth of the matter is that empaths will never engage in an intimate encounter with anyone who they don't love deeply, therefore any intimate activity will always be done out of love regardless of outward appearances. The important thing for any empath is to make sure they demonstrate their love for their partner on a regular basis through any means possible.

Parenting

Parenting is a challenging enough experience on its own, let alone when it involves an empath at one end or the other. Even so, every empath alive has grown up as a child with empathic abilities, and countless empaths start families of their own, thus entering the world of being a parent with empathic abilities. The increase of emotional awareness between parents and children can be both a blessing and a curse. It is therefore critical that you become aware of the dangers so that you can better manage the effects of your empathic abilities within your family relationships.

As a parent you will struggle with the flow of emotional input you receive from your children. This is made worse by the fact that children are usually full of conflicting and confusing emotions due to the biochemical changes their bodies are constantly going through. Needless to say, this only serves to increase the chaotic nature of the emotional input, creating a never ending whirlwind in your mind. It is essential that you develop the ability to detach from emotional input in order to protect yourself from becoming completely unhinged as a result of such heightened emotional stimuli. Practicing yoga or meditation on a daily basis can help make all the difference.

One of the positives of being an empathic parent is that you can sense when your children are suffering. This gives you an advantage of being able to make yourself available to them even when they are trying to hide their inner turmoil. Taken too far, however, this ability can turn into a form of privacy invasion, therefore only ever use it as a tool, never as a weapon. If your children refuse the help you offer you need to respect their privacy and let them deal with their situation on their own.

As a child you will find life somewhat more difficult because of your empathic abilities. Every child does things that they regret, things that often cause their parents a certain amount of pain and distress. However, most children are able to put those events behind them rather quickly, moving on to better times. Unfortunately, your empathic abilities will amplify the guilt and sorrow you feel for everything that causes your parents any sort of pain. Even the slightest of things such as a little white lie can cause you to feel absolutely guilt ridden since in addition to feeling your remorse you can also feel the pain your parents experience when you lie to them. This is highly unfair, of course, but it often results in empaths developing the highest of standards in terms of morals and virtue. Developing emotional detachment, however, is highly recommended in order to lessen the effects.

Work

Another environment that can impact an empath in a really big way is the workplace. This is particularly true for any job that creates a highly competitive atmosphere. In addition to experiencing their own stress and anxiety, empaths will also experience the stress and anxiety of those around them. This can result in an empath being ten times more stressed out than anyone else at any given time. Needless to say, this needs to be avoided at all costs.

The first rule for an empath is to create boundaries within the workplace. While the knee-jerk reaction is to offer help and solace to those in need, this can prove disastrous if no limits are established. As an empath you need to ensure that you get plenty of alone time to balance your energies and recharge your batteries. The heightened emotional atmosphere within the workplace will drain you faster than any other environment, therefore you need to take extra precautions to ensure your own health and wellbeing.

Perhaps the best case scenario is for an empath to find a job that allows them to be fairly autonomous. Although too much solitude can have its downside as well it can be a better challenge to face than that of being constantly mentally overwhelmed and emotionally exhausted. The important thing is to put your needs first at all times so as to prevent from becoming completely burned out and unable to perform your job adequately.

Extraordinary Perceptual Abilities

So far this chapter has focused on some of the more negative ways in which empathic abilities can affect your life. Fortunately, there are numerous positive ways in which your life can be significantly enhanced and enriched as a result of your inherent gift. As an empath you may find you have certain abilities that seem almost otherworldly at first. Rather than doubting or even fearing these abilities you should embrace them and develop them so that you gain every benefit that they have to offer.

One thing many empaths experience from time to time is the ability to see future or far off events. Commonly referred to as premonitions, these visions can happen quite unexpectedly, especially when the event doesn't impact the empath themselves. If you have ever seen a place or a person clearly in your mind, only to see that person or place on the news shortly afterward, you have had a premonition. This won't happen all of the time, and not all empaths have this ability. However, if you experience it you should embrace it for the miracle that it is. There probably won't be anything you can do to affect the situation, so don't feel as though you are somehow obligated to save the world. Instead, this is just a situation where your subconscious taps into the collective subconscious and discovers something interesting. The sooner you trust this ability is, the stronger it will become.

Enhanced dream states are another common phenomenon experienced by empaths. This stands to reason as dreams are born of the subconscious, just as emotions and intuition. Therefore, the stronger your skills of intuition and emotional sensing the more intense your dreams will be. At the very least you will have an increased ability to recall your dreams, something the average person usually lacks.

However, the chances are your dreams will also be richer in detail, more colorful and even longer lasting as well. Even better, you may experience what are called lucid dreams in which you become aware of the fact that you are dreaming. This opens up a whole new dimension that allows you to experience anything in the dream world with the same intensity as though it were occurring in the real world.

Finally, there are those empaths who have the ability to sense beyond human or personal experience. If you have ever 'read' the mind of an animal, or sensed the needs of a plant you are one of these people. The simple truth is that thoughts and emotions are pure energy by nature, therefore empaths can perceive them regardless of their origin. After all, a thought is a thought, regardless of whether it comes from a person or a tree. Therefore, it should be just as possible to read the one as it is the other. Many empaths don't possess this skill, however, that doesn't mean that their abilities are weaker or less developed. Rather, it's a matter of frequency. While some empaths are wholly tuned in to the human frequency, others are more in tune with the frequencies of nature. If you feel more at home with nature, and you can sense the needs of plants and animals, then this is how your empathic abilities affect your life.

In the end, each person's empathic abilities will affect their lives in different and unique ways. This is because each person's abilities are different, as are the lives they lead. Therefore, what is true for one person isn't necessarily true for another. As a result the most important thing you can do is to discover what is true for you and the methods that work best for you in terms of honing and harnessing your skills. The more in control of your skills you are the more in control of your life you will become. After all, being an empath doesn't have to be confusing and challenging, instead it can be something truly wonderful and fulfilling.

Chapter 5: Thriving as an Empath – Protect your Energy

Most empaths are driven to give of themselves in order to help restore the happiness and wellbeing of those around them. Unfortunately, this can lead to an empath becoming emotionally, physically and spiritually drained as a result. Even worse, empaths don't always have someone in their close inner circle that they can turn to for help in restoring their emotional energies. Subsequently, it falls on the empath to take the time and effort to protect and maintain their personal energy levels. This chapter will address some of the negative practices that you should give up, as well as some positive practices that you should start in order to take better care of your overall health and wellbeing. Additionally, it will provide some methods that will help you to stay emotionally grounded at all times. By following these recommendations you will not only be able to avoid becoming run down and emotionally drained, you will actually be able to start thriving as an empath.

Bad Practices to Give Up

As an empath the chances are you have developed a number of habits that serve to undermine your happiness and wellbeing. These habits aren't necessarily bad behaviors, rather they are good behaviors that have no boundaries. This is because empaths usually lack the ability to say "no," meaning that good, noble traits such as being giving and selfless can become all-consuming. Subsequently, it is important to recognize and eliminate these practices in order to maintain your emotional balance, health and overall wellbeing. Bad practices to give up include:

- **Always trying to please others.** Needless to say, trying to please others isn't a bad thing unto itself, however, when left unchecked it can create a situation where an empath over-commits themselves. By always saying "yes" to others you allow yourself to be used continuously, never giving yourself the time and space to restore your energy levels. The result is that you become drained and spent, much like a cell phone that isn't charged regularly. One of the most difficult yet important lessons to learn for any empath is to put their needs first from time to time. After all, you can only help others when you are strong enough to do so. Therefore, by looking after yourself you are ensuring that you can be of service to others.

- **Being an enabler.** Another bad practice that needs to be eliminated from your behavior is that of being an enabler. Unlike trying to please others, however, this behavior truly is bad in nature. The reason why it's easy to enable others to behave badly is that, as an empath, you can relate to why they need to behave badly. Unfortunately, not only does this not help the other person, it also serves to harm you as well. After all, most of the bad behaviors you enable involve how the other person treats you, meaning that by enabling them you only allow more harm to come your way. Therefore, it is essential that you recognize bad behavior when you see it, and rather than enabling it you take a stand and protect yourself from it. You can forgive and accept someone without actually encouraging their negative side.

- **Carrying other people's burdens.** This is a behavior that affects almost every empath at some point in time. Whenever you see someone else suffering, as an empath you feel the need to alleviate that suffering. In the event that you can't actually find a solution to what is creating the suffering you take on the burdens of others in order to make their lives better. While this seems like a good idea at first it actually is quite the opposite. First, it results in you taking on more burdens than you can handle. In the end, each person should only ever have to carry their personal burdens and no more. The second reason this is a bad behavior is because it enables the other person to continue going in the wrong direction as they don't have to carry the burden of their consequences. Ultimately, you have to let others experience the pains and burdens in their life in order to learn their lessons accordingly.

- **Always taking the blame.** One of the strongest traits of an empath is the unwillingness to cause harm to others. Unfortunately, this trait can result in an empath always taking the blame for when things go wrong, even when they aren't at fault. This can create several problems, both for the empath and for the other person involved. By always taking the blame you allow the other person to avoid accountability for their actions, thus enabling them to behave badly over and over again. Doing so robs them of learning valuable life lessons. Additionally, by always taking the blame you carry the burden of responsibility for other people's actions and wellbeing. The weight of such responsibility will eventually prove too heavy, leaving you crushed under its weight.
- **Feeling obligated to spend time with others.** Another behavior that appears positive but is actually harmful

is feeling obligated to spend time with others. This can significantly rob you of valuable alone time in which you recharge your emotional batteries, thereby leaving you vulnerable to emotional fatigue and even depression. Furthermore, you may wind up spending time with people who are highly negative, resulting in your energies being drained and damaged by their negative energy. In order to protect yourself you need to avoid such obligatory behavior, making choices that benefit you instead.

- **Being addicted to victimization.** Sometimes when an empath allows themselves to be victimized over and over again they begin to become defined by the process. After a while they identify with always being drained, depressed and taken advantage of. This can become so ingrained that when an empath begins to feel strong and happy they feel guilty, almost as though they aren't fulfilling their purpose. It is important to remember that your purpose is never to be victimized.

Therefore, such things as happiness and wellbeing should be normal for you, not the exception to the rule.

- **Giving energy to those who take it for granted.** This is one of the main ways in which an empath allows themselves to be victimized in the first place. By giving your time, effort and emotional energy to those who take it for granted you will only ever drain your resources with nothing to show for it at the other end. It's a bit like trying to fill a bucket with a huge hole in it. No matter how much water you put in, the bucket will always demand more. Eventually you need to learn to let go of those who take you for granted so that you can give your energy to those who will appreciate it, and thus be more effective as a result.
- **Being codependent.** This goes hand in hand with the previous point. When you remain in a relationship where the other person takes and never gives you will spend all your energy and never get anything in return. Needless to say, this will leave you in a constant state of

feeling drained and even depressed. It is critical for an empath to only maintain relationships that are mutually beneficial. Only then will the time you spend with others restore your energies. Any relationship that is one sided needs to be ended for your happiness and peace of mind.

Good Practices to Start

Discovering and ending bad practices is only half the formula when it comes to creating a life in which you can thrive as an empath. The other half of the formula is to discover and practice those behaviors that benefit you. Again, as an empath you have an increased responsibility to protect and maintain your energies, therefore it is absolutely essential that you perform those practices that will enable you to do so. The following list includes some of the more effective practices that will help you to stay strong and happy under any circumstances.

- **Accept your empathic ability.** As already mentioned in this book, being an empath is not as simple as it is often portrayed. One of the most difficult challenges any empath faces is accepting their empathic abilities. Not only can these abilities be confusing, they can also be distressing if you don't know what they are. However, once you realize the nature of your abilities it is vital that you accept them so that you can align your mindset with them. Learn to hear your inner voice and to trust what it tells you. Only then can you rid yourself of the inner conflict that so many empaths face.

- **Own your gift.** Accepting your empathic ability is only the first step toward creating a rich and fulfilling life. The second step is to own your gift. This is where you take the time to nurture your abilities so that they serve to improve your life. One thing many empaths fail to recognize is that their empathic abilities are for their benefit as well. You shouldn't feel as though you are only meant to improve the lives of those around you. Instead, you should constantly use your abilities for your benefit as well. Learn to discern those you can trust from those you can't, and protect yourself accordingly. Furthermore, use your intuition to know which paths will lead to failure and which paths will lead to the success you so richly deserve.

- **Develop emotional detachment.** Due to the sensitive nature of being an empath, it is vital that you learn to develop emotional detachment. This is the mindset where you can recognize the emotions of those around you without being affected by them. Buddhism and other similar traditions promote emotional detachment as a method of avoiding suffering. By engaging in such practices as meditation and mindfulness techniques you can develop the ability to detach yourself from even the most negative emotional environment, thus protecting you from the harm such negativity would cause.
- **Meditate on a regular basis.** Meditation is probably the most proven technique with regards to developing emotional detachment. Therefore, you should take the time to find a form of

meditation that best suits you. Not all forms are the same, therefore if you don't take to one simply let it go and try another. The important thing is that you find one that works for you. Not only will the right meditation help you to become detached, it will also help you to balance your energies, thereby releasing any stress that has built up due to exposure to negative people or circumstances.

- **Practice shouting, running and other forms of catharsis.** Another way to release stress and anxiety due to being exposed to negative energies is to expend it physically. Any high energy activity will help to burn off excess energy, including stress and anxiety. Running or engaging in any intense exercise is a great way to achieve this goal. A less physical alternative is to release energy through such methods as shouting or screaming. These practices allow you to express your emotional intensity, thereby restoring balance and inner harmony. In the end, any form of catharsis that allows you to expel excess or chaotic energy will help to keep you centered and balanced.

- **Develop somatic mindfulness.** Sometimes an empath can lose touch with their personal emotions due to the constant flow of emotions from the outside world. This results in them not attending to their own needs. One way to overcome this is to develop somatic mindfulness. This is a technique where you focus on different parts of your body to determine your emotional state. A tense jaw, for example, is indicative of stress and anxiety. An elevated heart rate can point to anxiety or even anger. Shallow breathing, stiff shoulders and clenched fists can also point to anger, stress and other negative emotions. By taking the time to assess your body you can determine your true emotional state, and thus take steps to correct any imbalances you are experiencing.

How to Stay Grounded as an Empath at All Times

Staying grounded is something that most empaths have a hard time doing. One reason for this is that they don't take the time to look for or recognize the signs that indicate when they are ungrounded or unbalanced. Even worse, most don't even know what such signs look like. Another reason is that they don't know how to restore balance and stay grounded even when they do recognize the warning signs. This section will discuss how to recognize and read those signs, as well as some proven methods for staying grounded and restoring emotional balance and wellbeing. Signs of being ungrounded include:

- **You have difficulty concentrating and staying focused.** This is a sign of emotional and mental fatigue in general, affecting both empaths and non-empaths alike. As an empath, however, you will probably experience this sign on a more regular basis as your emotional state will tend to become chaotic more often than in the case of an average person. Subsequently, any time you experience this condition it is important that you take the time to step back and evaluate your emotional state. Rather than trying to push through you need to take action to restore your emotional balance and wellbeing.

- **You find yourself being generally clumsy.** In addition to affecting your mind, being ungrounded can also affect your body in a very real way. This can take the form of being overly clumsy, even to the point of bumping into things such as furniture, doorways and even walls. Essentially, this is the same chaotic state for the body as confusion is for the mind. Thus, it points to the condition of being ungrounded. If you experience such bouts of clumsiness it is important to recognize the warning signs and take steps to restoring your peace of mind.
- **You struggle to remember details.** Memory is another mental skill that is directly impacted when you are ungrounded. This doesn't necessarily mean that you can't remember such things as your name or the day of the

week you are in, rather it means you can't remember more detailed information, such as appointment times, people's names and the like. Needless to say, many people struggle with details to one degree or another. However, if you struggle to remember certain things even after several reminders it may point to a state of emotional imbalance.

- **Reality and fantasy become hard to distinguish.** The more extreme the state of being ungrounded is, the more extreme the symptoms will become. One example of this is the inability to differentiate between fantasy and reality. In the event that you expect unrealistic responses to your words or actions, or you fail to grasp the particulars of your day-to-day life you need to take a serious time out and restore your mental and emotional wellbeing. This break from reality is the result of being too fixated on your inner world. Left unchecked, the consequences can be quite dire.

- **You find it difficult to complete tasks on time.** Few people can claim to be punctual all of the time, however, when an empath becomes ungrounded this behavior can become quite extreme. In a way, this is related to becoming detached from reality. The inability to recognize and follow time is another sign that you are too focused on your inner reality, thus causing you to be less in touch with the reality of the outside world. If left unchecked, this behavior can also become quite dangerous, causing all sorts of negative consequences in every area of your life.
- **Other people have a hard time understanding you.** If you have ever spent large periods of time alone you know that your first conversation with another person will usually be labored and even confused. This is because you have become so internalized that your external forms of communication have become wholly unnecessary. If this happens when you aren't alone it probably suggests that you are becoming ungrounded and that you

need to take the time to reorient yourself with the outside world around you.

The following are seven effective ways for grounding yourself:

1. **Drumming.** Drumming is a highly effective way of restoring your connection to the outside world. One reason for this is that it actually serves as a calming and restorative influence. The rhythm of a drum resembles a heartbeat, which creates a natural vibration that brings order to emotional and mental chaos. Furthermore, it can create the comforting sense that a mother's heartbeat has on her unborn child. Another reason why drumming can restore grounding is that it can provide a cathartic release of stress and anxiety, thus restoring balance to your heart and mind. Therefore, drumming can be highly effective whether you choose to simply listen to the rhythm or be a more active participant.

2. **Use essential oils.** Essential oils can help to ground you by shifting your focus to your physical senses. The sense of smell has been proven to be far stronger than previously believed, even challenging sight as the strongest of the five senses. Therefore, essential oils can bring you from your inner world back to the outer world in a fast yet gentle way. Furthermore, certain scents such as sandalwood, cedarwood, patchouli and peppermint have a calming and soothing effect, thus relieving the stress and anxiety that causes you to become ungrounded in the first place.
3. **Keep crystals on your person.** Crystals can help to restore your sense of being grounded by balancing your energies. Unlike drumming and essential oil methods, this method addresses the issue at the energy level itself. Crystals such as garnet, onyx, tiger's eye, hematite and copper have been shown to be effective in attracting positive energy, blocking negative energy or simply restoring the balance of energy. You can choose to keep such

crystals on your person simply by carrying them in your pocket or purse or you can incorporate them into jewelry, thereby adding a sense of artistic flair to your practice.

4. **Restore health and wellbeing to your root chakra.** This is another method that addresses any imbalance at the energy level itself. Taken from the Hindu tradition of chakras, or energy wheels, this method helps restore health and wellbeing to your root chakra which connects you to the Earth. You can restore energy by holding a hand over the area of your root chakra, right at the base of the spine, or you can surround yourself with the color red which will also help to increase vital energy to this area. The stronger this chakra is, the more grounded you will become.
5. **Practice tree exercises.** Most people only think of trees as being beautiful things that reach into the sky. The truth is that trees also reach deep into the Earth, spreading roots deep and wide in order to be strong and stable. Tree exercises, such as hugging a tree, will

help you to become grounded once again by helping you to connect to the Earth through the tree itself. Another exercise is to visualize yourself as a tree, with roots extending from your person to deep underground. This will help you to restore balance to your state of mind by bringing you from your inner self back to the world that is around you and under your feet.

6. **Consume energy rich foods.** Medical science has discovered a strong link between the energy of a person and the chemicals their brain produces. From their point of view, it is those chemicals that determine the nature of a person's energy. There are those, however, who would argue that the truth is the other way around and that a person's energy actually impacts how the brain works. Either way, the notion of the brain affecting energy opens up other options for restoring emotional balance and wellbeing. Certain foods, such as root vegetables, nuts, dark chocolate and protein rich foods can help create chemical reactions that

improve how a person thinks and feels. By eating these foods you can begin to feel grounded again almost instantly, especially in the case of dark chocolate.

7. **Find an exercise that matches your energy.** In the end, the main reason why an empath becomes ungrounded is an imbalance in their energy. This imbalance can be caused by a lack of energy, or alternatively, by an excess of energy. In either case certain exercises can help to restore balance by raising energy levels or by burning off excess, anxious energy. Running and martial arts can help to release any pent-up energy that causes a sense of being ungrounded. Gentler exercises, such as riding a bike or practicing yoga, can help to increase or simply realign energies, thereby restoring a person's overall health and wellbeing. The important thing is to pick the right exercise for the right time. For example, riding a bike, while beneficial, won't necessarily burn off excess or anxious energy the same way that running or martial arts would.

While each of these methods serves to restore emotional balance when you begin to feel ungrounded they can also serve to prevent issues from arising in the first place. The best way to ensure this is to implement some or all of these practices into your daily routine. Once you discover the practices that help you the best you should engage in them even when you are feeling strong and well. This will enable you to stay grounded at all times, thus helping you to develop a lifestyle that allows you to thrive as an empath, which is nothing less than what you deserve!

Conclusion

Now that you have read this book you will have a deeper understanding as to the nature of being an empath. Having empathic abilities can be very challenging, however, with a greater understanding of your skills you will be able to control their impact on your life more effectively. Furthermore, by implementing the methods discussed in this book for becoming more grounded you will be able to avoid the pitfalls that many empaths encounter as a result of letting their abilities go unchecked. The simple truth is that being an empath is a wonderful thing, however, it requires extra effort, awareness and skill. Hopefully this book has provided you with the tools you need to get the most from your empathic abilities. The very best of luck to you as you begin living the life of a truly empowered empath!

Sources

https://consciouslifenews.com/7-effective-ways-to-keep-yourself-grounded/1183716/

https://www.thoughtco.com/traits-of-empaths-1724671

https://www.amandalinettemeder.com/blog/2014/7/31/13-signs-you-are-an-empath-and-what-it-means

https://www.mindfulnessmuse.com/mindfulness-exercises/increase-somatic-awareness-with-a-body-scan-mindfulness-exercise

http://www.soulandspiritmagazine.com/signs-you-are-ungrounded/

https://theknowing1.wordpress.com/2011/07/01/at-a-glance-30-traits-of-an-empath/

https://www.psi-zone.net/signs.html

https://www.aconsciousrethink.com/2746/17-survival-tips-for-empaths-and-highly-sensitive-people/

https://www.learning-mind.com/types-of-empaths/

https://www.dictionary.com/e/pop-culture/empath/

CPSIA information can be obtained
at www.ICGtesting.com
Printed in the USA
BVHW080406271221
624869BV00008B/332